BREAKING  FREE

FROM

ANGER &

UNFORGIVENESS

Charisma
HOUSE
A STRANG COMPANY

LINDA MINTLE, PH.D.

BREAKING FREE FROM ANGER AND
UNFORGIVENESS by Linda S. Mintle, Ph.D.
Published by Charisma House
A Strang Company
600 Rinehart Road
Lake Mary, Florida 32746
www.charismahouse.com

Unless otherwise noted, all Scripture quotations are from the Holy Bible, New International Version. Copyright © 1973, 1978, 1984, International Bible Society. Used by permission.

Scripture quotations marked NAS are from the New American Standard Bible. Copyright © 1960, 1962, 1963, 1968, 1971, 1972, 1973, 1975, 1977 by the Lockman Foundation. Used by permission. (www.Lockman.org)

Scripture quotations marked NLT are from the Holy Bible, New Living Translation, copyright © 1996. Used by permission of Tyndale House Publishers, Inc., Wheaton, IL 60189. All rights reserved.

Cover design by Debbie Lewis
Interior design by David Bilby

Library of Congress Catalog Card Number:
2002108794

International Standard Book Number:
0-88419-895-2

This book is not intended to provide therapy,
counseling, clinical advice or treatment or to take
the place of clinical advice and treatment from
your personal physician or professional mental
health provider. Readers are advised to consult
their own qualified healthcare physicians regard-
ing mental health and medical issues. Neither the
publisher nor the author takes any responsibility
for any possible consequences from any treatment, action or application of information in this
book to any reader. Names, places and identify-
ing details with regard to stories in this book
have been changed to protect the privacy of individuals who may have had similar experiences.
The people referenced consist of composites of a
number of people with similar issues, and the
names and circumstances have been changed to
protect their confidentiality. Any similarity
between the names and stories of individuals
described in this book to individuals known to
readers is purely coincidental.

03 04 05 06 — 8 7 6 5 4 3
Printed in the United States of America

Anyone can become angry— that's easy. But to be angry with the right person, to the right degree, at the right time, for the right purpose and in the right way—that's not easy.

—ARISTOTLE

CONTENTS

"He better not cross me again."

"I feel like I could hurt someone."

"I'm out of control."

"I can't stop yelling."

"It seems like every little thing makes me mad."

"I hate the way I act when I'm angry."

"I AM SCARING THE KIDS."

"I find myself cursing when I get mad."

"I feel so ashamed."

"I can't believe I hit my wife. It will never happen again."

"When I get angry, all I see is RED!"

INTRODUCTION

Sound familiar? After all, everyone gets mad now and then. Anger is just a part of being human, isn't it? Of course! But if anger is causing problems in your relationships, job or everyday life, it may be time for a change. If you feel out of control or as if anger is ruining your life, read on. If you feel ashamed and guilty about the way you react when anger rises, keep reading. Or if you claim to never get angry, you are just not being honest! Anger happens. The good news is that it can be managed and even dissipated. You can break free from the potential negative effects of anger and live a peaceful life.

CAN YOU RELATE?

Jared just stared at his feet. He felt awkward and embarrassed. As he nervously glanced around my office, he finally spoke, "I've never been to one of *you types* before. I'm not crazy you know." His voice sounded desperate as he struggled to maintain some dignity. "I'm about to lose my family because I can't control my temper. I don't know what happens to me. Something sets me off, and suddenly I'm yelling and cursing. I have no control. I just see red. The next thing I know, I'm screaming at my kid or my fist has gone through a wall. I've even hit people a few times. And now, look at me. I have to see a shrink."

Perhaps your anger has never led to a therapy referral, but you know it's way out of line. When you explode, you yell and say things you later regret; sometimes it feels like you're out of control. It doesn't take much for you to get worked up. You can relate to Ann. "I don't know what comes over me. It can be the smallest thing that irritates me. Then I explode. It doesn't matter who is around me. I just unleash these pent-up feelings and then feel terrible. Every time it happens I tell myself I won't react like that again, but I do. I can't seem to stop."

Or maybe you aren't sure if your anger

is really a problem. Yes, you get frustrated, but you've never *hit* anyone. You only yell once in awhile, usually when provoked. Rick expressed it like this: "It's not like I'm angry *all* the time. It usually takes something big for me to explode. One time I got so mad at one of my employees, I lambasted him with insults. Then I fired him. In truth, he needed to be fired. But I probably shouldn't have called him names and cursed the way I did. It was like a dam broke inside of me and all this anger spilled out."

Maybe you think you shouldn't be angry at all. Anger isn't an emotion you allow to surface because you think it is wrong and destructive. Belinda, for example, prides herself on the fact that she is a *peacemaker*. "I never get angry, only frustrated. Anger isn't part of my life. I find it distasteful. I don't raise my voice, and I don't get in arguments with anyone. As a Christian, I don't think I should be angry."

Whether you are seriously out of control, occasionally destructive, hot-tempered, irritated or unaware of existing anger, it's time to break free from anger's grip. In this book, you will:

- Understand this powerful emotion
- Examine biblical guidelines for anger expression
- Identify anger triggers
- Learn strategies for healthy anger expression
- Practice and live a transformed life

While it's impossible to eliminate all the people and circumstances that bring an angry response, it's not impossible to "be angry, and yet do not sin" (Eph. 4:26, NAS). In fact, it's your *choice* to respond to angry feelings in either a positive or negative way. Feelings will come and go, but you are always responsible for your actions.

BREAKING FREE

PRAYER FOR YOU

When I'm angry, help me not to sin!

CHAPTER 1

UNDERSTANDING ANGER

*Usually when people are sad,
they don't do anything. They
just cry over their condition.
But when they get angry, they
bring about change.*

—MALCOLM X

Anger is a powerful emotion. It can be a
signal for change. It can also be destructive
and cause problems in your personal relationships or place of work. What are your
ideas about anger and how it works? Take
this simple test to see how accurate you are
when it comes to understanding anger.

Anger and You

Circle true or false to these 10 questions:

T F 1. As long as I don't look or sound angry, I am not.

T F 2. If I ignore anger long enough, it will go away.

T F 3. If I punch something or throw something, I'll feel less angry.

T F 4. Anger is shameful and not nice.

T F 5. It's OK to keep the peace at any price. It's what God wants.

T F 6. If I express anger, my relationships will be in danger.

T F 7. Women don't get angry, just upset.

T F 8. Christians shouldn't get angry.

T F 9. God understands that sometimes I just can't control my anger.

T F 10. As long as I didn't mean to get so angry, I'm OK.

The answers to all ten questions are **FALSE**. These questions address common myths about anger. So what is the truth about anger, and how does one handle this powerhouse properly?

ANGER IS A POWERFUL EMOTION

Anger is a God-given emotion. Emotions are simply mood responses to living our lives. Our emotions may be unpredictable at times, but they are not good, bad or sinful. Emotions are simply a part of our human makeup, subject to our control. And they are strongly influenced by our thoughts, behavior and family relationships. So anger itself is not wrong. However, we can have a wrong *response* to anger.

You have a choice when it comes to how you will behave when angered.

THE POSITIVE SIDE TO ANGER

Not everyone has an anger problem. You can learn to express anger appropriately and use it in beneficial ways. You can manage anger and, better yet, learn to resolve it. There is a positive side to this emotion.

- Anger can motivate and lead to change. If anger is acknowledged and the root cause addressed, change occurs.

- Anger can help us understand our expectations and unmet needs. It can lead to direct expression of that need or expectation.

- Anger can give us the needed energy to deal with a dangerous situation or an injustice.

- Anger can be used to problem solve.

- Anger can be used to show you care about someone. For example, anger at a teen for disobedience is a sign of caring. Again, how you deal with that anger is important. Screaming your head off is not a sign of affection—it's a lack of self-control. Telling your teen how angry his disobedience makes you feel, and then setting an appropriate consequence, is an act of love. In this case, anger signals caring because it is an honest relationship expression that leads to correction. Correction given to those we love is often necessary for character development. It is God's way. As our loving heavenly Father, He often corrects us when we disobey or need to refine our character.

- Anger can motivate positive action in relationships. For example, the anger a wife has at an alcoholic husband can be used to set this boundary—"If you come home drunk and become physical with me, the police will be called."

- Anger can be directed at sin and the enemy's schemes. This leads to prayer and intercession. Jesus' anger reflected godly concerns, not selfishness or pride.

Notice that all these positive uses of anger lead, motivate or help us to do something. It's when we stay angry and refuse to do anything positive about our feelings that problems occur.

THE NEGATIVE SIDE OF ANGER

Most of us struggle with the negative fallout of anger. According to expert Charles Spielberger, a physiologist who specializes in anger, *anger* is defined as "an emotional state that varies in intensity from mild irritation to intense fury and rage." Anger creates a physical response that causes increased heart rate, respiration, blood pressure and release of energy hormones.[1] Perhaps this is one reason Psalm 37:8 tells us to cease from anger—it can cause bodily harm.

There are also several studies that link unresolved anger to emotional problems. In some cases, anger can be the underlying culprit for depression, anxiety, eating disorders and other mental health conditions.[2] So aside from your spiritual state, both your health and mental health are at stake. Other negative consequences from poor anger management include:

- Major and minor relationship problems

- Negative thinking and acting out

- Verbal, emotional, sexual and physical abuse

- Crime and violence

- Abuse of power and control, often at the expense of others

- A sense of entitlement
- A cover-up for emotional hurts and wounds
- Self-focus on desires, selfishness
- Pride
- Hate, hostility, bigotry, rage and aggression

I'M NOT ANGRY, JUST FRUSTRATED!

"I'm not angry, just frustrated!" (Or add your own favorite substitute—upset, irritated, disappointed.) I once counseled a dad who spent weeks trying to convince me that he never got angry, only frustrated. His bulimic daughter nearly vomited every time he downplayed his anger. She experienced his rage at home even though he wouldn't admit to it. As a result, this made her mad, but she wouldn't tell her dad how angry she was because she feared his response. Her dad's anger was intimidating. He was in a position of authority and could hurt her with his words.

So instead, she dealt with her anger indirectly by bingeing and vomiting. She turned her anger inward toward her body—a safe target. She would swallow her anger and binge after every angry encounter with her dad. Then she would vomit. Over time, she developed bulimia. Her eating disorder didn't improve until her father came to grips with his anger and its impact on his family. The root cause of his anger was important to determine. It turned out to be related to the constant criticism he received from his father. Unconsciously, he was acting like his dad—criticizing his daughter and flying into rages when she wasn't "perfect."

The dad had to stop slinging all his past emotional wounding at his present wife and daughter. Anger made him feel powerful, not hurt. Hurt was "not allowed for men." But his hurt was big, as was his unforgiveness toward his father. Once he chose to forgive his father, let go of the past and take responsibility for his behavior, his anger dissipated. This helped his daughter directly address her upsets, and consequently the eating disorder lost its power over her life.

Do you think some people are more prone to anger than others? Are you one of those people? Does it seem like you have a low tolerance for frustration? Does any little thing annoy or frustrate you? Have you wondered why this is? Consider this. Some children seem to be born more edgy and irritable. They cry often and appear easily frustrated. As toddlers, they are cranky and prone to upset. One thought is that genetics or physiology predisposes some people to more anger.[3]

Try this word association. When I say "angry," do you think of men or women? Most of us associate anger with men more so than women, but we all know women get angry. Let's not forget Shakespeare's Lady MacBeth or the biblical Jezebel who didn't hesitate to kill a host of prophets (1 Kings 18:4)! Women have anger problems, too. But men and women do have anger differences when it comes to biology.

Due to brain differences, men and women view anger-producing situations differently and choose different responses.[4] Women tend to have a wider range of emotional responses to anger. Men are more likely to experience anger, then get over anger more quickly, but be more aggressive in the process. Aggression is also influenced by higher levels of testosterone in men.

In addition to genetic predisposition, your family, as we saw in the story above, is also a source for *learning* how to manage anger. A family that is disruptive, chaotic and doesn't know how to handle anger creates angry people. You learn what you see. If family members are out of control and possess few skills to manage their anger, you tend to behave the same way. Or if family members don't express anger and keep it bottled up, chances are you will, too.

A third influence is the culture. Role models in movies, television, music and other media are hardly good examples of healthy anger expression. We witness people throwing things, yelling, getting their way at the expense of others, being abusive, wrestling people to the ground, shooting others and using force, inflicting pain, becoming violent, seeking revenge, feeling entitled to anger and basically letting it all hang out. The message is that anger is sanc-

You alone are responsible for your anger responses.

tioned, especially for boys and men. Anything goes when it comes to releasing those pent-up feelings. Women, on the other hand, are expected to be the "kinder and gentler" sex. Typically women have more problems with being assertive and swallowing anger.

However you've been influenced, you alone are responsible for your anger responses and will be held accountable. If you are prone to explosions in which you hit, break things, seek revenge or verbally abuse others, you have an anger problem and need help. Or if you are depressed or physically ill because you harbor angry feelings, it's time to make changes. Anger should not become destructive to you or others.

In summary, anger is a normal part of

our complex emotional makeup. We learn how to express anger from parents and other role models. Anger can be used to make positive changes or be unleashed in hurtful ways. Since anger expression is learned, the good news is that it can be unlearned. This means change is always possible.

BREAKING 🕊 FREE

PRAYER FOR YOU

Lord, help me to admit that I have an anger problem. Then change me as I acknowledge I am responsible for my behavior and accountable to You.

CHAPTER 2

ADMIT
YOU HAVE
A PROBLEM

The evil in this world is committed by the self-righteous who think they are without sin because they are unwilling to suffer the discomfort of significant self-examination.

— SCOTT PECK

*H*ow do you know if your anger is a problem? Circle "Yes" or "No" to these twenty-five questions. If you answer *yes* to any of these questions, you need to make changes.

Y N   1. Is anger controlling or dominating me?

Y N   2. Do I physically hurt myself or others (e.g., hit, slap, shove, kick, threaten with a weapon or words)?

Y N 3. Do I feel like I have to defend myself most of the time?

Y N 4. Do I lash out at others with criticism or sarcasm?

Y N 5. Do I have difficulty listening to others?

Y N 6. Do I often berate another person (e.g., fault find, name-call, accuse of wrong doing)?

Y N 7. Do I have flashes of temper that seem uncontrollable?

Y N 8. Do I find myself apologizing over and over for anger instances?

Y N 9. Do I engage in malicious gossip, stealing or trouble-making?

Y N 10. Do I insult others?

Y N 11. Do I feel disgust or contempt for anyone or any group?

Y N 12. Am I overly suspicious?

Y N 13. Do I constantly blame others?

Y N 14. Do I have feelings of revenge and judgment?

14

Y N 15. Am I argumentative and irritable?

Y N 16. Am I constantly challenging someone?

Y N 17. Do I harbor resentment, jealousy or envy?

Y N 18. Am I uncooperative and disruptive?

Y N 19. Do I appear unsympathetic to certain groups or people?

Y N 20. Do I hold on to unforgiveness?

Y N 21. Do I argue just to argue?

Y N 22. Am I withdrawn or silent about my feelings?

Y N 23. Do I think I have an anger problem?

Y N 24. Do other people think I have an anger problem?

Y N 25. Do I like the power I feel when I get angry?

Not only will this list help determine if anger is a problem for you, but it will also identify specific areas to change.

GETTING AT THE ROOT OF ANGER

The best way to completely resolve anger is to get at the root of the problem. Have you been hurt or emotionally wounded?... The victim of rage or aggression?...A target for physical, verbal or sexual abuse?... Chronically upset or disappointed?...A storehouse for unforgiveness? Review the following list of possible anger roots, and see if any apply to you. If they do, your anger will continue to be a problem until you resolve the root issue.

B R E A K I N G F R E E

M E N T A L   H E A L T H F A C T

Possible Root Causes of Anger

1. Unmet expectations

2. People let you down

3. A lie you have believed about yourself or others

4. Physical, sexual or verbal abuse

5. Angry thoughts

6. Feelings of entitlement

7. Injustice

8. Unforgiveness

9. Fear/anxiety

10. Impulsivity and lack of self-restraint

11. Trauma or loss

12. Neglect

13. Unwillingness to accept blame or responsibility

~~~~~~~~~~

If you are unable to resolve anger problems alone or with the help of family and friends, then I encourage you to get counseling and/or deliverance—whichever applies to your situation. Don't be afraid to look behind your anger and see what is lurking there. It's your hope for freedom. Ignoring the root cause is like putting a Band-Aid on a wound that never heals.

Before we move on, there are a few other important points to be made.

Don't make excuses for your anger.

Don't try to explain your anger with these excuses: "My dad hit me first." "I'm Irish

(or German, or…) and have a temper."
"My wife makes me so mad." "She deserved
it." Too often we blame others for our angry
reactions—"He made me so mad." No one
makes you do anything. You aren't forced
into anger by anyone. Your angry reaction is
up to you. You decide how you will
respond. Most often inappropriate
responses are habits, practiced for years.
You alone are responsible to change your
reaction if it is inappropriate.

One of the biggest excuses I see in men
is to blame others for their violent behavior. There is no excuse for violence. Blame
is a pathetic way to deal with a problem. I
don't care how upsetting someone's behavior is; it is not license to misbehave and sin.

Don't jump to conclusions.

Is your anger based in a real situation,
or is it based on your perception of that
situation? Sometimes we misread people
and judge them to be hurtful when they
aren't. You may need to clarify a situation
and get more facts. Go to the person and
ask him what he meant, and then tell him
how his behavior affected you. Find out if

he was really trying to hurt you.

At other times we may put ourselves in someone else's place and ask, "What would I have done in that situation?" Perhaps the person is going through a stressful time and is easily upset or tired. She may need the benefit of the doubt or just a break from a caring person.

We also need to consider the developmental phase of the angry person. For example, very young children are not good at expressing a range of emotions. They will often act in extreme ways and say, "I hate you."

You can respond by saying, "I love you, and you are just angry because I said no." Then teach the child how to handle his anger in a good way. Unfortunately, many adults don't know how to handle their own anger.

Does anger cover up some other emotion?

Most often anger is a cover-up for hurt and pain. It is a powerful protection against being vulnerable and hurt again. It's much easier to get angry than to feel

19

hurt. So look behind the anger, and you may find fear, insecurity, vulnerability, pain or some other emotion. For example, when I was a guest expert on a national TV show discussing teen violence, there was a number of teens who wanted to kill and hurt people. It quickly became evident that these teens were badly wounded by absent fathers who neglected them or were in jail or simply not around. When I started talking about absent fathers, the teens teared up and started to cry. After a few moments of feeling vulnerable and scared, they reverted to angry talk. Their pain was big, and they were afraid to feel it. Anger, on the other hand, made them feel powerful and in control.

PRAYER FOR YOU

Forgive me, Lord, for uncontrolled anger and sinful responses. Reveal to me the root of my anger problems so I can break free. If there is emotional hurt behind my anger, show me, and heal that hurt. If I have believed lies that have led me to be angry, reveal Your truth.

CHAPTER 3

ANGER IS A BIBLICAL REALITY

Refrain from anger and turn from wrath; do not fret—it leads only to evil.

—PSALM 37:7–9

Let's begin by dispelling the notion that anger is not part of the Christian walk. Anger is a biblical reality. God tells us that He gets angry. In the Old and New Testaments there are more than seventy-five references to the anger of God. Most often His anger is provoked by idol worship and disobedience. (See Psalm 106; Jeremiah 8.) Fortunately for us, He is slow to anger and gracious in mercy—two things He directs us to be as well.

Anger in the Bible

If you are wondering about human anger, check out these biblical accounts:

- *Cain* slaying Abel (Gen. 4:5–8)
- *Simeon* and *Levi*, on account of the humbling of their sister, Dinah (Gen. 49:5–7)
- *Pharaoh*, toward Moses (Exod. 10:11, 28)
- *Moses*, toward Israel (Exod. 32:19; Num. 20:10–11)
- *Balaam*, toward his donkey (Num. 22:27, 29)
- *Balak*, toward Balaam (Num. 24:10–11)
- *Ephraimites*, toward Gideon for not soliciting their aid against the Midianites (Judg. 8:1)
- *Jonathan*, on account of Saul's persecution of David (1 Sam. 20:34)
- *Saul*, toward Jonathan (1 Sam. 20:30–34)
- *Ahab*, because Naboth would not sell his vineyard (1 Kings 21:4)
- *Naaman*, because Elisha directed him to wash in the Jordan (2 Kings 5:12)

- *Asa*, because the prophet reproved him (2 Chron. 16:10)
- *Ephraimites*, toward Judah (2 Chron. 25:10)
- *Uzziah*, toward Azariah the priest because of his reproof (2 Chron. 26:19)
- *Ahasuerus*, toward Vashti (Esther 1:12)
- *Haman*, because Mordecai did not salute him (Esther 3:5)
- *Ahasuerus*, toward Haman (Esther 7:7)
- *Elihu*, because Job had beaten his friends in argument (Job 32:3)
- *Moab* (Isa. 16:6)
- *Nebuchadnezzar*, on account of the insubordination of the three Hebrews who refused to worship his idol (Dan. 3:13, 19)
- *Jonah*, because the gourd withered (Jon. 4:1–2, 4, 9)
- *Herod*, toward the wise men who deceived him (Matt. 2:16)
- *People of Nazareth*, toward Jesus (Luke 4:28)
- *Jews*, against Stephen (Acts 7:54–58)
- *Paul*, toward Ananias (Acts 23:3)[1]

Given all these instances of anger, there should be no doubt in your mind that anger is an important emotion with which we must contend. The biblical examples tell us how people dealt with their anger. Did they rule over it, or did it rule them? Our *response* to angry feelings is what matters to God.

When Jesus took the form of man and lived on the earth, He experienced a wide range of emotions, including compassion, pity, grief, anguish and, yes, anger. The Pharisees, who continually tried to trap Him in their legalism and refused to recognize Him as the Messiah, angered Him. He was angered by the money-changers in the temple for making God's house a den of thieves, and He overthrew their tables. His anger related to *godly concerns* rather than *self motives*.

> *When you are angry—stop, think, listen and calm down before you react.*

The directive, "Be angry, and yet do not sin" (Eph. 4:26, NAS), affirms anger as part of our human nature. Since it is usually the mishandling of anger that creates problems, God adds, "Do not sin." We are to control this powerful emotion and use it productively. Anger must not lead to harm or take root in our hearts. If it is denied, held in or allowed to build up, it can easily turn to resentment, hatred or revenge. For instance, in the case of Cain, anger led to murder—an obvious sin. We would agree that anger expressed in abusive ways, whether verbal, sexual or physical, is sin. The struggle most of us have is with less violent forms of anger expression like criticism, gossip, wishes for revenge or harm to a wrong doer. If we are honest, our response to anger often needs work.

SCRIPTURAL DIRECTIVES ON ANGER

Because God understands us intimately (He created us), He addresses our emotions in His Word. Commit to memory these scriptural directives for handling anger. Later, you will be given strategies for success. It's one thing to know the guidelines and another to *do* what they say.

- *"Be quick to listen, slow to speak*

and slow to become angry...do not let the sun go down while you are still angry" (James 1:19; Eph. 4:26). Your impulse may be to lash out. Instead, slow down and think before you act. Things spoken hastily can be regretted later. Words cannot be taken back. When you are angry—stop, think, listen and calm down before you react. Deal with your anger immediately if possible. Don't let it fester. Don't bury anger. Unresolved anger can lead to destructive and explosive behavior.

- *Don't give full vent to your anger* (Prov. 29:11). You may be angry, but this doesn't give you permission to unleash your anger on anyone or anything. Control your tongue and your behavior. Self-control is a fruit of the Spirit. Cursing, hitting, breaking things and intimidating others are not godly responses. This scripture tells us to restrain our instinctual response.

- *Stop and think* (Prov. 14:17; 15:1–2; 16:29). A quick response in anger is often regretted. Don't react immediately. Give yourself time to think, calm down and line up your reaction according to Scripture.

- *Don't get caught up in name-calling* (Matt. 5:22). This is straightforward—blaming, name-calling and bullying are not Christlike behaviors.

- *Don't take revenge on a violator* (Rom. 12:19; Heb. 10:30). Our society is big on revenge and law-suits. The Lord says that vengeance is His, and He will repay (Isa. 63:4). You will not receive much reinforcement from the larger culture for this position, but it is scriptural.

- *Forgive those who anger you* (Matt. 6:14). You are to forgive others as Christ has forgiven you. It doesn't matter if you are justified in your anger. It doesn't matter if others are wrong. Forgive. You didn't deserve His forgiveness, but He gave it to you anyway. Now do the same for others.

- *Get to the source of your anger* (Ps. 4:3–5; 139:23–24). Search your heart. Be honest. What are you harboring? Whom are you judging? Ask the tough questions. Listen in quiet meditation for God to speak to you.

- *Don't stay angry* (Col. 3:8). This is critical. Feel the anger, try to resolve it and then move on. People get physically and emotionally ill when they hang on to anger and allow it to develop roots of bitterness.

- *Give the anger to God* (1 Pet. 5:7). It may be a cliché, but the Word tells us to cast all our cares on Him. Tell God. Pour out your emotion to Him. He can handle it.

- *Don't take offense* (Prov. 12:16; 19:11). Try to overlook insults and not take offense. The natural response is to retaliate or to obsess on the insult. Refuse to do this.

- *When possible, don't associate with angry people* (Prov. 22:24). The concern here is that you will become like them or be negatively influenced.

- *Gain control over a quick temper*
  (James 1:19; Prov. 14:17, 29;
  16:32; 19:19). A hot temper gets
  you into trouble. Impulsive behavior must be controlled.

At this point you may be thinking, *I've
read those biblical guidelines a million
times, but I just can't seem to do them.*
Don't give up. Knowing what the Bible has
to say and changing behavior are two sep-
arate things for most of us. The rest of this
book will teach you success strategies. God
doesn't tell us to do something and then
fail to equip us to do it!

B R E A K I N G F R E E
P R A Y E R F O R Y O U

*Help me to be obedient to Your Word
and to make necessary changes. In
You all things are possible. I choose
to believe I can become the self-
controlled person You desire me to
be. I can break free from anger.*

CHAPTER 4

IDENTIFY THE TRIGGERS

The unexamined life is not worth living.

—SOCRATES

*T*he first step to overcoming anger is to admit that anger is a problem. You can't change something you don't admit! Then, the next step is to identify the triggers that set you off.

A trigger is a *cue* that a behavior follows. An emotion like anger usually comes as a response to something that happens or to a thought you have about an event or person. For example, you may get angry when your teen breaks the curfew rule (the trigger is the breaking of a rule or the thought of broken trust). You may get angry with your boss for piling up work with no extra pay (the trigger may be a thought of injustice). Or you may become angry when you think your spouse is being inattentive (the trigger is a thought like *I'm not important to her* or the fact that she doesn't speak to you when you come home from work). Thoughts and/or behaviors can trigger angry feelings. Your job is to identify triggers that set off an angry reaction in you.

BREAKING 🐦 F R E E

MENTAL HEALTH FACT

Common Triggers for Anger

- *Specific thoughts*—Example: *That was unfair. How dare she do that? He is hateful. No one cuts me off on the road.*

- *Situations*—Example: An injustice, unfair treatment, partiality, cheating, lying

- *People*—Example: A mother-in-law, an abusive parent, an alcoholic uncle, a boss

THE AUTOMATIC ANGER METER CHART

Think about these three categories, and see if they apply to times when you have been angry. Then, the next time anger arises, begin an Anger Chart using the form on page 37 to track your anger. (There is a sample chart on page 35 to show you how to use it.) Briefly describe the thought, situation or person who angered you. Write down a few descriptive words under the first column ("Trigger") of the Anger Chart. What led you to feel angry? What thought did you have? Who was involved? Two examples are given.

Next, in the "Automatic Thought" column, write down the first thought that comes into your head about the anger event. Don't edit your thought or change it because it may sound a little irrational. Just write down what comes in your head.

Then, under the column labeled "Anger Meter," identify the emotion you felt and rate how intensely you felt it on a scale from 1–10 (1 being a very mild feeling of anger and 10 being the most intense anger you can imagine or have felt).

Next write down what you did (the behavior) as a response to the angry feeling. Did you hit, yell, swear, leave the room, refuse to speak, blame someone or become critical? Be very specific and not vague like, "I blew up." Describe your behavior.

Copy the Automatic Anger Meter Chart on page 37 and use it as a tracking form. Keep a record for a few weeks or long enough to record at least ten to twenty instances of anger. Once you begin writing down anger triggers, you should see a pattern. If you cannot identify a pattern, it may be that your anger is easily aroused and any number of things set you off. If that's the case, you will need to revisit possible roots of your anger and work more on those specific issues first. For people who are easily angered at many different things, counseling is recommended to help identify the roots of anger.

For most people, a pattern emerges when they track angry feelings. For example, anger is aroused every time you have lunch with your father, every time an

Anger Chart A
Automatic Anger Meter

Sample Answers

Trigger (What happened)	Automatic Thought	Anger Meter (Emotion & Intensity) 0–10	Behavior (What you did)
Wife complained that I forgot to take out the trash.	She's always on me.	Irritated (6)	Yelled and called her a name.
Passed over for a promotion.	My boss hates me.	Angry (8)	Threatened to quit.

35

expectation goes unmet or when your thoughts about a situation become hopeless. Whatever the pattern, pay attention to it. It will help you to prevent an angry response in the future. Sometimes just being aware of triggers is enough to behave differently, because you can anticipate the situation and plan your response ahead of time. Prayer can be given to the specific issue. Ask God to help you deal with anger in a healthy way. (See anger strategies in chapter seven.)

THREE WAYS TO DEAL WITH ANGER TRIGGERS

Here are three ways to deal with anger triggers once you have identified them:

1. Avoid the triggers.

You can't always avoid an anger trigger, but sometimes you can. If you know that some thing or some person upsets you, and you don't have to put yourself in the situation or be around that person, then don't. For example, let's say that playing basketball and losing the game sets you off. Then one way to work on your anger is to take

Anger Chart A
Automatic Anger Meter

Trigger (What happened)	Automatic Thought	Anger Meter (Emotion & Intensity) 0–10	Behavior (What you did)

a break from the game. Find a new hobby. Or when a complaining coworker works you up into a fit during lunch breaks, go to lunch with someone else.

Of course this strategy may only be a temporary solution and isn't always possible. You can't always avoid an anger trigger. For instance, when your mother-in-law tries to run your life, you can't get rid of her! Well, you could, but I don't recommend it! Instead you have to work on responding to that trigger in a new way.

2. Practice a new way to respond to anger triggers.

When you know the trigger and can see it coming, practice a new response *before* the incident happens. For example, Jerry tracked his anger for two weeks. He noticed a pattern. Every morning when his boss stopped by his desk to check to see if he was at work on time, Jerry got angry. He felt insulted (gave it a 7 on the 1–10 Anger Meter). He was a grown man and never had problems getting to work on time. It angered him to be checked on like a school kid. Since he didn't want to change jobs, he couldn't avoid the situation. So he decided to change his reaction and practiced it with me in therapy. "Tomorrow when he comes to check on me, instead of seething under my skin, I'm going to look at him, smile and say, 'I notice you stop by every morning to see me. Is there anything I can help you with? I'm sure your time is valuable.'"

I pretended to be the boss (with Jerry's coaching), and he practiced this new response. Armed and ready, he tried the new response the next morning. After he asked the question, his boss looked rather surprised and said, "Uh, no. Looks like everything is under control." He also stopped coming to Jerry's desk every morning. This strategy may not work for every anger occurrence, but it's worth a try. In Jerry's case, it was an easy fix to his problem. Chapter seven will outline several additional strategies from which to pick. An Anger Response Menu is provided.

3. Pray for self-control before you encounter the trigger again.

Another way to use the Anger Chart is to note what sets you off and then begin to pray about those events, persons or thoughts. Ask God to help you stay calm and, by His Spirit, to give you the self-control He promises as a fruit of the Spirit. Remember that the fruit of the Spirit is "love" (Gal. 5:22). The Word says to love our enemies and pray for them (Matt. 5:44). This is not easy to do unless you have an intimate connection with your Father God. Draw close to Him, and ask for the eyes and ears of Christ. Ask Him specifically to help you see each person and event as an opportunity to be a witness of the supernatural love of Christ. Prayer is a powerful tool to equip you to handle any circumstance.

Let's review so far:

1. *Admit you are angry* (chapter two). Don't deny the emotion and engage in "anger insteads" such as overeating, boredom, depression, anxiety, physical illness or gossip.

2. *Identify the source* (chapter two). What makes you mad? What is the root cause? Usually someone does something or says something that hurts you.

3. *Know the biblical guidelines for anger* (chapter three).

4. *Identify anger triggers* (chapter four). Use Anger Chart A to track anger instances.

5. *Look for patterns* (chapter four).

6. Once you've identified the triggers, *try three strategies* if possible:

   - Avoid anger triggers.
   - Rehearse and practice a new response to those triggers.
   - Anticipate the situation, and pray for self-control before you encounter the trigger again.

BREAKING  F R E E

PRAYER FOR YOU

Let me see the patterns to my anger so I can begin to react in new ways. Through prayer, I am trusting You to empower me.

CHAPTER 5

CALM DOWN AND STOP THOSE ANGRY THOUGHTS

No man can think clearly when his fists are clenched.
— GEORGE JEAN NATHAN

*A*nger is a part of life. You can't control everyone and every circumstance around you, so you must learn to react in ways that aren't destructive to you or others. No matter what the source of your anger, find ways to control and resolve it.

WHAT NOT TO DO!

For years people have encouraged angry people to release it physically—punch a pillow, throw something, scream loudly in your car. Research tells us that such an attempt is not a good idea. When people lash out with angry behavior, it actually escalates the anger.[1] Contrary to popular advice, physical release of anger doesn't make you feel better. Acting out makes you more hostile!

The way we deal with anger can be put into three general categories: anger that is…

- Calmed
- Suppressed or hidden
- Expressed

Of these three general anger actions, which one is the best and gets an A for effectiveness?

"Just calm down."

Isn't calming down the best approach? You know, "Jim, settle down. Get control of yourself. It will be all right." So Jim takes a deep breath and tries to relax. Eventually the inten-

Acting out makes you more hostile.

sity of his anger leaves him. He is no longer highly aroused by an angry feeling. Not a bad strategy. Jim didn't hurt anyone and was able to calm his physical body so as not to endanger his health. The problem is that Jim never dealt with the issue that made him so mad. But he was able to control his outward behavior and his inward body responses. Jim gets a B+. He controlled himself, but never dealt with the root cause.

"Just don't get angry."

Karla hides her anger. She holds it in, tells herself to stop thinking about it and then tries to think about or do something positive. She works on redirecting her anger so as not to feel it. Most of the time this strategy works, although lately she has felt depressed, and her blood pressure is up. Her therapist thinks she has pushed her anger deep inside. Lately she's been more irritable with the kids. Karla gets a C because her strategy doesn't always work. Keeping her anger inside is affecting her health and her relationships without resolving the problem.

Sue doesn't express anger and needs to learn how. Instead, she gets back at people indirectly without telling them why. She claims she is not angry at all when asked about her anger. Sue has lost friendships because of this *passive-aggressive* approach to dealing with anger and people. She releases her anger indirectly, not in an honest up-front way. Sue gets a D- because she denies she is angry (she really is) and then attacks in indirect ways (passive-aggressive). She can't deal with the root cause of her anger when she is so busy denying she even feels this emotion. And her passive-aggressive anger is hurtful to others and pushes them away.

"Just let it out."

Tim is aggressive. He expresses himself in ways that attack others when he is annoyed or offended. He feels powerful and in control when he gets angry. Others back off and are intimidated by him. Although Tim gets his way, his methods are ruthless. He scores the big F for dealing with anger. Tim is just a big-kid bully. His anger is never used to solve any problems.

Ron works hard to express his anger in a healthy way. He's not aggressive, but assertive. He avoids blame and emotionally charged words and simply states what behavior made him mad and why. He then tells the person what he needs and tries to negotiate getting his needs met. There is no criticism, cynicism, hostility or pushy demands. People don't always give Ron

Work on direct expression of anger and try to resolve the problem.

what he wants or needs, but he has learned that he can't control others. He can only control his anger response. He tries to be respectful of others, direct and assertive, not aggressive. Ron gets an A for effort and effectiveness. Most of the time, he can resolve the problem.

Anger expression, when done appropriately, lowers your physical arousal and emotional feelings. So don't hold anger in, deny it exists, or suppress it. And certainly don't lash out in angry aggression. As we learned, this doesn't calm you down. It actually increases your anger. Instead, work on direct expression of anger and try to resolve the problem. You'll get an A in life.

DEAL WITH ANGRY THOUGHTS

Before I give strategies to control anger

and resolve it, there are two areas that may first require practice—your thoughts and anger arousal.

In therapy I usually ask, "When you got angry, what were you thinking about?"

The typical answer is, "I didn't *think* anything. I just *felt* angry."

And I reply, "Yes, you did think something. You just weren't aware of it."

Thinking influences feeling. Thoughts often cue up anger. Anger is an intense emotion that leads people to yell, curse and say things they often regret. Behind that red-hot feeling is a "thinking" that you know who contributes to your emotional state.

Usually your thoughts go like this: *I'll never... He'll always... How dare she...? My life is over... How could he...? I can't believe... I ought to... No one treats me like... The nerve of... Can you believe...? He'd better... I won't take... How unfair... This is an insult... He should have...* Angry thoughts often come when we demand things from people—"He'd better not treat me this way." Well, guess what? He just did.

Continuing to think you didn't deserve what happened doesn't help you feel better. And it certainly does little to fix the problem.

We all get upset when things don't go our way or people treat us poorly, but thinking negative thoughts just upsets us more. Instead of demanding that people behave "the right way," try changing your thoughts. Think, *I wish I could control people, but I can't. I'm not going to let this get to me. It's not the end of the world. It's frustrating, but I can handle it. How I respond to this injustice is more important because God will hold me accountable for that.* Acknowledge your disappointment, but don't rev yourself up with negative thoughts of revenge, injustice, hopelessness and drama.

If you can "take each thought captive," you can lessen the rage you feel or even prevent it from happening. (See 2 Corinthians 10:5.) Anger is influenced by thoughts. Remember, we have thoughts all the time whether we are aware of them or not. I'm asking you to become aware of your thoughts and start listening to them.

You can stop thoughts and change them. Do your thoughts line up with Scripture, or are you thinking revenge, hate, aggression or even violence?

THOUGHT STOPPING

Practice what therapists call *thought stopping*. It is a practical way to renew your mind. Negative and angry thoughts play on each other and often lead to aggression, violence and other negative behavior. Thought stopping can be used to deal with those negative thoughts. It is simple in concept, harder to apply.

When an ungodly or violent thought comes into your head, interrupt your stream of thought. Silently yell "Stop!" and force yourself to think on something else or do something to startle yourself in order to stop the thought—pinch yourself, snap a rubber band on your wrist, get up or take a deep breath. Then refocus your thoughts on something positive.

Philippians 4:8 tells us to think on positive things. Think about things that are true, noble, just, pure, lovely, of good

49

report, virtuous, or anything praiseworthy. List the blessings in your life, the times of answered prayer, the testimonies of others, a kind deed or the beauty of creation. If you think for a few minutes, you can always find something positive to focus your thoughts on because of who God is. Thinking about problems and negative things often leads to depression and feelings of hopelessness. If we know the character of God and His promises, we always have hope.

Now, I know that it isn't natural to think about God in the middle of an angry moment. God or anything positive is the last thing you are thinking about. But that is the point. If you want to break free from anger, you must make changes. *Change is not easy and requires you intentionally to do something different.* When you stop something negative (in this case, angry thoughts), you have to replace them with something positive (positive thoughts). It's hard to stay angry and escalate a fight when you purposefully focus on God's love and/or the power of the Holy Spirit in you to overcome this difficulty. In fact, when you think about who you are in Christ, it may remind you that you have the power to overcome evil and sinful behavior. Remind yourself that your weapons of warfare are spiritual.

The next time you feel really angry, try to stop and identify the thoughts that preceded that angry moment. Then work on changing those

Change is not easy and requires you intentionally to do something different.

thoughts. Instead of obsessing on the way someone acted or the injustice done to you, choose to think about your true defender, Jesus Christ. He goes before you like a shield and is present to protect you and your reputation. No one can take that away from you.

DEALING WITH PHYSICAL AROUSAL

I've already mentioned that anger affects your physical state. So not only do you have to learn to take charge of your thoughts, but you also need to teach yourself to calm down. There are several things you can do to train yourself to reduce physical arousal when you feel angry. If you practice these exercises daily for about twenty to thirty minutes, you can successfully use them the next time anger rises inside of you.

Deep breathing

When you are angry, your breathing becomes more rapid. One way to slow down that physical response and reduce your anger is to take deep breaths very slowly. Simply inhale slowly and deeply through your nose and breathe from your abdomen or diaphragm, pause a few seconds, and then exhale slowly through your nose or mouth. Do this ten times or until you calm down. Sounds very simple. It is! Practice this when you are *not* angry so you'll know what to do when an anger situation arises. It will calm you.

Deep muscle relaxation

The opposite of tension is *relaxation*. It is impossible to be out of control with anger when you are physically relaxed. So, practice tightening and then relaxing each of your muscles. For example, clench your fists, hold the tension and then relax. Do this with muscles around your face, neck, shoulders, arms and back until you feel the tension in your body subside. Tighten a muscle group, hold the tension and then relax. If you practice muscle relaxation before going to bed or the first thing in the morning, you will be able to use it when you get in an angry situation and need to relax your body. You should practice daily until you can cue your body to relax fairly quickly. Then the next time you become angry, tense and relax your muscles until you feel calm enough to handle the situation.

Think on things that are good

If anger has you "seeing red," then refocus on a pleasant visual picture. *Before* you encounter an angry time, think of a pleasant scene that is calming to you. Do this before an anger incident occurs because it is hard to think up a peaceful scene in the middle of experiencing an intense emotion like anger.

Some people like to picture a beach with

palm trees; others feel serene in a cabin nestled in snowy mountains. Still others picture Christ sitting by them, or they imagine heaven. Whatever makes you feel peaceful and calm, get that scene in your head and think about it until you feel more relaxed.

When anger hits, you might need a time-out from the moment in order to visualize this scene. That's OK; just say, "I need a minute to calm down." Close your eyes, and visualize yourself in the middle of your peaceful place. Take a few minutes to visit this place in your imagination. It will calm you.

Practice Makes It Work

I can't stress how important it is to practice thought stopping and relaxation. These reactions won't come easily at first. It takes real concentration to stop a negative thought and take it captive. It may be difficult, but it will get easier with practice. It also takes an act of your will to focus intentionally on a peaceful scene, slow down your breathing or tense, then relax your muscles rather than allow anger to build. But with practice, you can make these responses become second nature. You are changing your habit of exploding. It takes time.

It may be helpful to find someone to whom you can be accountable for your thoughts and/or behavior, especially if you've been out of control habitually. You might need to be coached and encouraged or just need help implementing the steps in this book. In addition, you will benefit from prayer with a group of people who care about you. Your goal is to exhibit more of the fruit of the Spirit—love, joy, peace, longsuffering, kindness, goodness, faithfulness, gentleness and self-control (Gal. 5:22).

There are a number of places to get help for anger problems if you find yourself unable to do the things in this book. Support is an important part of making any major change in life. Many community mental health centers or family service agencies offer anger control groups. Look for local community workshops, church seminars or classes on anger management. Check out books on the subject or talk to other men and women about how they handle angry feelings. Read your Bible, and ask God to help you take "your thoughts captive" and calm your physical body. Never say, "I can't." Because of God and His Holy Spirit, we have been made new, and all things are possible. Discouragement does not come from God. It comes from the enemy of your soul. He wants you defeated. God wants you to break free!

BREAKING FREE
PRAYER FOR YOU

Lord, help me to take every thought captive as Your Word directs me to do. Help me to exhibit the fruit of Your Spirit living in me so that I might exercise love and self-control.

CHAPTER 6

SETTING THE STAGE FOR CHANGE

Let us not look back in anger, or forward with fear, but around in awareness.

— JAMES THURBER

I can't change. This is who I am. Take it or leave it. Someone else will accept me for me." Have you or someone you know used this excuse when it comes to anger? Let's not forget that change is the hallmark of the Christian experience. When you asked Christ into your life, you were immediately transformed to a new creation. "New" is the operative word here. "New" implies a change from the "old" way you thought, behaved and related to people. Because we aren't perfect people, change is an ongoing process. It has to be worked through the help of the Holy Spirit.

Pray for God to change your heart. You need to be softened to the things of God. To do this, get into the Word, pray and worship God. I know this sounds like a simple idea. It is. Application is far tougher.

Ben had a terrible anger problem. His rage stemmed from living with an abusive father who criticized and belittled him as a child. Now Ben hated the way his anger unleashed on his wife, Beth. He sought therapy to help identify the hot buttons for his anger and to learn anger control strategies.

Ben also asked God to help him. He studied scriptures on anger and self-control. He knew how he was supposed to behave with his wife. Ben worked in therapy to learn anger cues and strategies for self-control. When his anger was aroused, he practiced the strategies and prayed. As he worked to calm himself down, he asked the Holy Spirit to give him the self-control he needed for the moment. He knew that without the help of the Spirit, lasting change was a question mark.

Ben was determined to get his anger under control, but he lived eight years with Beth before he had a change of heart. His wife feared Ben's anger. He never hit her, but he came close. Ben was physically intimidating. Beth's fear was grounded in reality. His anger was historically out of control.

As Ben began making changes and exercising self-control, Beth kept silent. In therapy she said she was glad her husband was changing, but she didn't trust the change to last. I encouraged her to share this with him. Ben was upset that his wife wasn't more positive. This wasn't easy.

What Ben failed to recognize was the full extent his threatening behavior had on the relationship. A few weeks of appropriate anger control did not wipe out eight years of history. Beth had reason to be hesitant. She needed to see sustained change. And Ben needed to recognize how his behavior created Beth's uncertainty. He was frustrated by Beth's unenthusiastic response and ready to give up. Why should he try if his wife didn't recognize his efforts?

I gave him three reasons to try:

- Even if Beth never said a word to him, his behavior was still wrong.

- Beth's behavior did not determine his.

- He didn't understand how his past influenced the present.

I told Ben to stop looking to Beth to affirm what he should have learned years ago—to control his temper. Yes, it would be great if she would pat him on the back, but under the circumstances he should understand her hesitancy. He needed to reinforce his own behavior. He was doing the right thing. Anger control was a sign of a healthy man. He should pat himself on the back for making this change. But to expect Beth to be his biggest fan at the first sign of change was asking too much. She had been traumatized by his past behavior and was just now allowing herself to lower her guard. Over time, as Ben demonstrated consistent change, she would relax and have positive words for him. Patience was needed here.

In the next session, Beth told Ben that she was very happy he was controlling his anger. But she still worried that he might resort to past behavior. Ben apologized for not understanding how his anger created fear. He now realized how his behavior hurt Beth. Ben took responsibility for his actions, knowing his actions had created a relationship problem. Immediate reinforcement for change would come from self and those working with him on anger control. He couldn't blame his wife for her lack of immediate response. He had to prove himself trustworthy.

The real question was, "What was motivating Ben's change?" Did guilt, Beth's fear, the therapist, the threat of divorce or something else *Change is usually progressive.* motivate him? Hopefully he was motivated by his sin. He recognized his behavior was not Christlike and that it had harmed his relationship.

Change is usually progressive. If you are the spouse of an angry person and can encourage him or her along the way, do so. It helps tremendously. Patience is greatly needed on the part of both spouses, and patience is not a valued virtue in our society. Our disposable culture says that if something doesn't measure up immediately, discard it and move on. Don't give up. Change is hard work, but you can break free.

ANGER TIPS

In order to break free, you must be ready to change. Here are ten ways to begin:

1. Don't be easily offended.

Many times we choose to take offense even though none was intended. Give people the benefit of the doubt rather than continuing to question their motives and presume they mean harm. There are people who willfully hurt and have a pattern of provocation and destructive behavior. But at other times we read negative intent into situations because of our past woundings. Give mercy as often as you can, and assume the best rather than take offense. It's your choice.

2. Refuse to keep thinking about the injustice.

Once you've identified the source of your anger, work to resolve and release it. Too often we obsess over injustices and continue bringing them up. Futilely we embrace unforgiveness. In fact, unforgiveness leads to bitterness and health problems. (See chapter eight.)

3. Don't vent.

As I stated before, research actually shows that when you express anger by screaming, yelling, punching pillows, raging or throwing a tantrum, you actually increase anger rather than reduce it. Venting does not make anger go away.

4. Deal with each angry incident when it happens.

Don't allow anger to build up or take root. Bitterness will result. As hard as it may be, try to resolve the anger-creating problem as soon as possible. Don't avoid the problem.

5. Resist the urge for revenge.

Revenge is a natural response, but not a godly one. Ultimately, God will deal with every person for his or her behavior. Remind yourself that revenge is God's and not yours. If you give mercy, you'll also receive it. Keep in mind the Bible tells us that as long as the earth remains, there will be seedtime and harvest (Gen. 8:22). If people sow deceit and misdeeds, they will always reap a harvest from that seed.

6. Determine not to raise your voice.

Practice talking in a calm voice so as not to escalate a conflict. A loud or raised voice can intimidate and set up a defensive reaction from the other person. Yelling scares people and often says you are out of control.

7. Deal with underlying feelings of insecurity, low self-esteem and past woundings.

If you don't take care of the feelings that lurk under the anger, they will continue to resurface. Angry people often suffer from insecurity. Anger makes them feel powerful and in control. In addition, depression can be rooted in unresolved anger. Get counseling if you need more help to determine the root of your anger.

8. Don't say or do things impulsively or according to how you feel.

The Book of James clearly says the tongue has power for life or death. (See James 3:1–12.) Words hurt and can't be retracted. If you are really angry, don't speak or act until you can calm down. (See chapter five.)

9. Have a regular physical outlet for built-up stress and frustration.

It's important to add physical exercise to your life. Exercise and playing sports help release stress that can lead to anger and irritability. An appropriate physical outlet like running, racquetball, tennis or other sports helps release built-up tension. Walking, hiking, riding a bike and rollerblading with your kids are good sources of exercise. Excessive stress without relief makes us irritable and edgy.

10. *Agree to disagree.*

If you have acted appropriately and made several attempts to resolve an angry situation, yet there appears to be no solution, agree to disagree. You may have to accept that things are not the way you like or want them. You can't force others to change.

B R E A K I N G   F   R   E   E

P R A Y E R   F O R   Y O U

Lord, no excuses. I need to change and can't depend on others to make it happen. Help me to set the stage for change—have a soft heart, read Your Word, repent from the sin of anger, be empowered by Your Spirit and move into freedom.

CHAPTER 7

BREAK-FREE STRATEGIES

Anger is a momentary madness, so control your passion or it will control you.

—HORACE

You need new ways to respond when angered. It is best to try and resolve anger, not just manage it. Here are specific strategies to help break free from anger; they're not in any particular order. Think of them like a menu from which you can choose. When you are angry, practice one of these new responses.

As you learn and practice, it helps to use the Anger Chart once again (chapter four). In this chapter we will add two more columns. (I have included a sample chart on page 83 to show you how to use it.) I recommend you make copies of the chart on page 85 to track your progress. The two new categories are *Renewed Thought* and *New Behavior*.

THE ANGER RESPONSE MENU

From previous chapters:

- Change the situation that triggers anger
- Thought stopping
- Deep breathing
- Deep muscle relaxation
- Think on things that are good
- Exercise
- Agree to disagree

More strategies (this chapter):

- Anger rules
- Be assertive
- Talk to someone
- Employ cool-down tactics
- Develop humor
- Be empathetic
- Use restraint
- Pray
- Change your self-talk
- Change your friendships

- Reduce or eliminate violent media
- Write a letter you don't send
- Establish an anger contract
- Rehearse and practice
- Forgive (see chapter eight)

ADDITIONAL ANGER STRATEGIES

Establish and observe anger rules.

If you don't have anger rules, make them now. They will help you resolve problems without getting sidetracked or out of control. If you slip up and violate a rule, ask for forgiveness and go back to your list. If you have trouble following the rules, take a break, review a written copy and revisit the issue at hand. If you have a history of unfair fighting, write down the rules and have them in front of you.

For example, I work with a couple who has a rule that neither party will threaten divorce when angry. This couple has a long history of using this threat as a power play. It is very hurtful and brings up feelings of rejection and abandonment from previous marriages. Threatening divorce does nothing to resolve a problem. It only adds to already bad feelings. The rule against using divorce as a threat is a good one for all couples.

Other typical fair fighting rules are listed below.

B R E A K I N G  F R E E

M E N T A L   H E A L T H F A C T

Fair Fighting Rules

- No name-calling, swearing, bringing up past problems, shouting, physical contact, threats, blame statements, use of drugs or alcohol or yelling.

- One issue should be raised at a time without reference to past problems.

- Both parties need to be in control and relatively calm when trying to resolve an issue, or wait until one or both can demonstrate this.

- Stick to the issue at hand.

Learn to be assertive, not aggressive.

If you are angry, it is important to say so, but you must learn to say it in a way that can be heard. Don't acquiesce to the situation and then feel angry later. Or don't use aggression to bully or intimidate. Neither is a good strategy. Instead be assertive. This means ask for what you want, say *no* if it is warranted and take responsibility.

Start by saying you are angry, but do so using "I" statements. Then follow up with a request for change. For example: "I feel angry right now. I don't want to fight. Instead I'd like to come to some agreement on weekend visitation."

An assertive response is one in which you say how the problem affects you, express your feelings, then make a request. Being assertive doesn't mean the other person will automatically do what you say. They might not, but at least you handled your anger in a constructive way. That's all you are responsible for, remember? Example: Say, "I get so angry when I see your clothes lying all over the house. Please pick them up," instead of, "You make me so mad. You are a slob."

Don't apologize for your feelings, and

don't feel guilty asking for change. Your feelings are what they are—not right or wrong. You want to be able to resolve problems rather than just control your anger. When you request change, it also helps to state the consequences you expect. "When you pick up your clothes, I feel you care about me and the house." Or, "When I come home from work and you give me a kiss, I feel loved."

Often, anger wells up inside us because we don't say *no* when we should. Instead we agree to things against our better judgment, and then store the anger away. Learn to set limits and politely say, "No thank you." Example: "I really don't have the energy to go out tonight. I'm going to pass." At times, you may have to be firm setting limits and not cave in to manipulation.

If you are someone who swallows feelings, learn to speak them out in "I" statements. If you are an exploder, work on controlling your impulse to lash out. Learning to be assertive will avoid anger buildups, physical problems and explosions. Follow this simple formula and fill in the blanks:

B R E A K I N G   F R E E

M E N T A L   H E A L T H F A C T

Use "I" Statements

I feel _____

when _____

because _____ .

~~~~~~~~~~~~~~~~~~~~~~

The more assertive you become, the less angry you will be. If you need help learning and practicing assertiveness, attend a seminar or course. Work with a therapist who can help you develop this skill.

Talk to someone about your anger.

Women, more so than men, often find relief when they talk out their anger. Talking makes them feel heard and helps them to think through the anger experienced. Talk but don't obsess. Find a friend or trusted person with whom you can talk.

Others (more often men) find that the more they talk about anger, the angrier they become. They don't want to relive the experience and are prone to more aggression when they do. However, talking can help identify your feelings. Often, people realize that behind anger are hurt and pain. Anger is often a cover-up for more vulnerable feelings. Talking out your feelings with a safe and neutral party differs from direct, explosive, face-to-face yelling or attack.

It is important to know if this strategy works for you. If you benefit from talking it out with someone, do it. Just remember that talking about anger doesn't solve the anger problem with the person involved.

Employ cool-down strategies.

We've already discussed ways to calm down your body (chapter five), but here are more ideas for those angry moments.

1. *Count to ten.* If you are in the habit of responding quickly and impulsively, force yourself to count to ten slowly so you have time to think before you act.

2. *Take a time-out if you need one.*
   We give time-outs to children so
   they can stop and think and then
   go back to the situation with
   more self-control. Adults can
   benefit from this strategy as well.

3. *Temporarily walk away* from the
   situation, but come back once
   you are calm and ready to
   resolve the problem. Don't just
   walk away and do nothing. The
   key word here is *temporary*,
   which doesn't mean walking
   away for hours or days. Take ten
   to thirty minutes.

4. *Be empathetic.* Empathy can be
   learned. It's the process of putting yourself in someone else's
   shoes. When you get angry, you
   may be thinking of the injustice
   done to you. Try thinking about
   what the other person is going
   through or must be feeling. Life
   is not all about you. See the
   other's point of view, pain or
   hurt, and love them with the love
   of Christ. Empathy reduces
   anger.

5. *Develop a sense of humor.*
Humor diffuses anger. I'm not suggesting you laugh off problems or make fun of serious things. But you can use humor to break the tension. One person I know is able to make a verbal picture when someone calls him a name. For example, he was once called a "block head." He made a visual picture of that and started to laugh. It totally diffused the angry moment. Both people started to laugh when he reported what he saw. Then, they went back to the issue at hand without the tension.

6. *Pray.* When you're frustrated, irritated, angered or upset, take a deep breath and pray. Ask God to give you the self-control you need for that very moment. Ask Him to fill you with His love and help you to exercise the fruit of the Spirit. Have regular sessions with God. He is always available and will listen to your feelings of injustice. He knows them so well because He experienced them while living on earth. He was

mocked, lied about, spit on, physically abused, shamed and born into a lowly family. He knows what you feel. Nail those feelings to the cross. He died to set you free. Prayer is transforming.

7. *Use restraint.* This involves learning to hold back your anger until you have it under control. Relationships benefit tremendously when we restrain ourselves from responding impulsively. Because words cannot be taken back and impulsive anger leads to a lack of trust, practice restraint by using the relaxation techniques already outlined.

8. *Change your self-talk.* Our self-talk fuels the fire of anger. When we change our self-talk from critical and negative to hopeful and merciful, we change. For example, if every time your wife denies you sex, you think to yourself, *I have a right to have sex. How dare she?*, you are going to be angry. If instead you say, "I need

to find out what the problem is
because this is difficult for me
and going to cause me to be
upset," you won't be so angry.
Change those thoughts to something more reasonable, positive
and forgiving.

9. *Problem solve.* Reacting is much
easier than taking time to solve a
problem. Anger should be a signal that something needs your
attention. If the problem is your
own impulsivity and quick reaction, then practice the cool-down
strategies and relaxation. If your
anger is aroused from interper-
sonal interactions, then try to
solve the problem instead of just
reacting. Make a plan, and check
your progress.

10. *Reduce or eliminate your consumption of violent media.* We
consume violence daily—through
television, movies, music and the
Internet. Media affect your
behavior. Aggression begets
aggression. We know from
numerous studies that watching
violence increases aggression and

that consumption of violent media negatively affects your attitudes and behavior.[1] If you are prone to anger, eliminate violent media.

11. *Change your friendships.* If you hang out with people who insult, call names and are prone to aggression, beware. It rubs off. Don't tolerate aggression and violence among your friends. Think about it. If your teenager goes out with angry kids, he tends to be more irritable and disrespectful. If you work with angry coworkers who let insults fly, it works on you as well. If you have an anger problem, find friends who don't.

12. *Write a letter that you don't intend to send.* Sometimes it is helpful to write a letter to a person who has been the object of your anger. The letter helps you get in touch with angry feelings and express them without worry of retribution, because you don't send the letter. Writing also helps you take responsibility for your reactions. I frequently use this

technique in therapy with people who have been sexually abused. The letter releases buried anger and allows for its safe expression. No one but you, and maybe a therapist, has to see it. God already knows what is in your heart, so you might as well acknowledge it.

13. *Establish an anger contract.* Make a contract. Come up with a reward each time you successfully control or resolve your anger. You can also add a negative consequence for when you lose control. For example, one client rewarded himself with a small amount of cash that went into a jar every time he was successful at anger control. If he lost control, a larger withdrawal was made. Every week, his account was a concrete evaluation of his progress.

PRACTICE, PRACTICE, PRACTICE

It's time to track your progress. Record several anger instances on your expanded Automatic Anger Meter Chart on page 85.

1. Look at the automatic thought column and review what you tell yourself about each anger incident.

2. Replace irrational or negative thoughts with more moderate positive self-statements and record it in the "New Thought" column.

3. Choose a new response from the anger menu. List it under "New Behavior," and practice it.

4. Take the anger incident that rates the lowest on your Anger Meter, and rethink the thought and a new way to response. See if you can stay calm. Then take the next lowest emotional incident and do the same. Practice imagining these events keeping your body calm. Then expose yourself to an anger trigger that rates low on the Anger Meter and see if it works.

5. With each success, expose yourself to triggers that are more and more difficult to handle. Each time, practice staying calm and controlling your anger. Don't expose yourself to things or people that

make you really angry until you can control your reactions. Think of it like an inoculation. Incremental exposure builds resistance, and success is just around the corner.

For example, Bill gets angry every time his wife tells him what to do. Later he feels bad about the way he handled the situation. His automatic thought is, *I'm a grown man. She thinks I'm incompetent.* He rates his anger a 3 on the Anger Meter. He reacts by purposely ignoring his wife's request. So Bill charts his behavior as it appears in the first four columns on the sample chart on page 83.

Bill sees the pattern and decides it's time for a change. So he comes up with a new thought that is more positive, empathetic and gives his wife the benefit of the doubt.

New thought

Bill changes his thought to, *Order is important to her. She's worried it won't get done.*

Anger Chart B
Automatic Anger Meter

Sample Answers

Trigger (Cue)	Automatic Thought (Old thought)	Anger Meter Emotion (Rate 0–10)	Behavior (Old response)	Renewed Thought (More rational)	New Behavior (New response)
She tells me what to do.	I'm a grown man.	Angry (3)	Ignore request	Order is important to her.	Be assertive
Ignores my hard work.	I can never please this man.	Mad (4)	Swallows his anger and drinks.	I get paid to do my job, and I do it well.	Deep muscle relaxation and prayer

New behavior

Be assertive. "Honey, please don't tell me what to do. I already know and will get it done tonight. I *feel* irritated *when* you give me directions *because* I know what to do."

Bill first practices this new way of responding in his head. Then he tries it out and works on staying calm using the cool-down methods. He is successful, and so moves on to another anger-causing situation, which he rates as more intense on his Anger Meter.

He notices from his chart that he gets angry when his boss doesn't comment on his hard work. Bill's chart now looks like the sample chart on page 83, including the last two columns.

Then Bill practices a new behavior from the anger menu: "Instead of swallowing my anger and reaching for a beer when I get home, I am going to practice deep muscle relaxation to calm my body and stay abstinent. God is the only one I have to please—not man. I know when I am doing a good job. I don't need to numb myself with alcohol."

Anger Chart B
Automatic Anger Meter

TRIGGER (Cue)	Automatic Thought (Old thought) 0–10	Anger Meter (Emotion & Intensity)	Behavior (Old response)	Renewed Thought	New Behavior (New response)

As you begin to substitute new reactions for old anger behaviors, read over the biblical guidelines given in chapter three. It is important that you incorporate God's directives in your plan. He desires you to imitate Christ in all you do.

BREAKING FREE

PRAYER FOR YOU

Lord, give me the strength and determination to make necessary changes. Help me to stay in Your Word and spend time in prayer so that the fruit of the Spirit can be evidenced in my life. It is possible to change my angry reactions and become more like You.

CHAPTER 8

FORGIVENESS

Forgiveness does not change the past, but it does enlarge the future.

—PAUL BOESE

*I*n every anger event there are three factors: what happens, the consequences and your response. Often we can't control what happens or the consequences that follow, but we do have control over our reactions. Our reactions have much to do with the state of our souls.

What is our greatest challenge when it comes to breaking free from anger? It is the command to forgive those who have angered us. In order to really break free, we have to release resentment and judgment we may hold over others.

The Bible is our guide for forgiveness. Forgiveness is not an option. Christ died to forgive our sins, and He commands us to do likewise. Love is the motivating ingredient in forgiveness. "Hatred stirs up quarrels, but love covers all offenses" (Prov. 10:12, NLT). Forgiveness is an individual act of the will. So pray for compassion and mercy.

It is your decision to hold on to past hurts, grudges or injustices. If you do, unforgiveness will plague you, resulting in bitterness and an unhappy life. And you certainly won't break free from anger.

You may be stuck emotionally because the person you need to forgive has not asked for it—and does not *deserve* it. Nevertheless, you still must forgive. Forgiveness benefits you as well as the one who hurt you.

Perhaps you are the one who needs forgiveness. Ask others to forgive you. When you do, confess the wrong you committed, and then turn from it. In other words, change your ways. True repentance involves turning from sin and embracing God's right way of doing things. He will give you power to make necessary changes as He works on your heart, attitudes, thoughts and character. He wants you to be more like Him, an imitator of Christ.

Let's look at the steps of forgiveness that lead to freedom.

1. *Choose to forgive.*

Because God forgave you, you too must forgive. But it's a choice. Did we *deserve* the forgiveness of Christ? No, but He gave it anyway. When we don't forgive, we become bitter and block the transforming power of Christ in our lives. It doesn't matter how many times the person has sinned against you or how severe the sin. (See Matthew 18:21–22; Luke 17:4; Ephesians 4:32; Colossians 3:12–13.)

2. *View forgiveness as an act of obedience to God.*

The Bible is very clear. When you obey God, there are blessings. When you don't, you set yourself up for problems. You will break fellowship with God if you allow unforgiveness in your heart. See yourself as a willing vessel of God's grace.

> Dear friends, never avenge yourselves. Leave that to God. For it is written: "I will take vengeance; I will repay those who deserve it," says the Lord. Instead, do what the Scriptures say: "If your enemies are hungry, feed them. If they are thirsty, give them something to drink, and they will be ashamed of what they have done to you." Don't let evil get the best of you, but conquer evil by doing good.
>
> —ROMANS 12:19–21, NLT

It may take a while for your feelings to catch up to your decision to forgive, and that's OK. Healing is not always immediate. Forgiveness does not mean acceptance of sinful behavior. You are not agreeing with what the person did. Rather, you are choosing to forgive.

3. *Remove past offenses from the mind.*

Don't continue to think about the wrongdoing.

No, dear friends, I am still not all I should be, but I am focusing all my energies on this one thing: Forgetting the past and looking forward to what lies ahead, I strain to reach the end of the race and receive the prize for which God, through Christ Jesus, is calling us up to heaven.

—PHILIPPIANS 3:13-14, NLT

4. *Meditate on Scripture.*

Forgiveness is not always easy. Our natural instinct is to retaliate or seek revenge. But as you meditate on the life of Christ and His Word, you will be encouraged and empowered to do the unnatural.

5. *Give your hurts to God.*

When anger is unleashed, it creates heartache. If you have been wounded by words or actions, do what Jesus did:

He never sinned, and he never deceived anyone. He did not retaliate when he was insulted. When he suffered, he did not threaten to get even. He left his case in the hand of God, who always judges fairly.

—1 PETER 2:22-23, NLT

6. Pray for the offender.

This may be the hardest step of all. Not only do you forgive, but you also release that person to the judgment of God. You do not have to judge him or her. God will. "As for me, I will certainly not sin against the LORD by ending my prayers for you. And I will continue to teach you what is good and right" (1 Sam. 12:23, NLT). We are called to pray for those who offend us: "But I say, love your enemies! Pray for those who persecute you!" (Matt. 5:44, NLT).

In some ways it is easier to forgive than it is to release judgment. Secretly we want the person to fail or to be chided for his or her wrongdoing. Ultimately, judgment is up to God, who is full of mercy and grace. Our responsibility is to pray for our enemies. It's radical but biblical.

If you are the one who has committed anger offenses, ask God to forgive you. Then accept His forgiveness. Don't walk in shame and guilt once you have truly repented (Rom. 8:1). God is faithful to forgive you (1 John 1:9). He will change your heart if you ask. He is merciful and willing to transform your life, but you have to submit to His ways. Remember—it is His desire that you break free from anger.

BREAKING  FREE

PRAYER FOR YOU

Lord, forgive me first for my own anger responses that were not in line with Your Word and did not show love and kindness to others. Then forgive me for not forgiving those who have angered me. I choose to forgive and release all judgment over them. Help me walk in Your grace and mercy as I remind myself how often You have shown me the same.

CHAPTER 9

BREAKING FREE
SUMMARY

*I*f you've read this far, it's been a lot to digest, right? Here is a brief review to break free from anger:

1. *You control your anger reaction.*
   Anger is a God-given emotion. It is not right or wrong, but the way you handle anger can be. Anger can be positive when it is motivated by godly concerns and not from selfishness or pride. The way you respond to anger is important. You will be responsible for your anger responses because they are subject to your control.

2. *Admit you are angry.* Since anger is God given, acknowledge it. It does no good to blame others or to pretend anger doesn't exist. The first step to freedom is to admit you have a problem.

3. *Follow biblical guidelines.* You must study the scriptures related to anger in order to know what God expects. Then commit to those guidelines and practice.

4. *Identify anger triggers and thoughts.* Track your angry behavior and learn what sets it off. Know the thoughts associated with anger. This is the key to breaking free. Renew your mind with the thoughts of Christ, and change your behavior to imitate Him.

5. *Lower your physical arousal,* and stop angry thoughts. Practice the techniques that develop new behaviors.

6. *Substitute new behaviors* from the Anger Response Menu. Choose appropriate anger responses to replace those that are destructive and out of control. The goal is to resolve anger when you can, but always manage your responses.

7. *Forgive yourself and others.* Forgive yourself for out-of-control anger thoughts and behavior. Do

not live in condemnation. Self-forgiveness is based on Christ's sacrifice on the cross and His redemption. Repentance requires a change in behavior, a turning from sin to righteous living. In addition, forgive others whether or not they ask for it or deserve it. God forgives; so must you.

8. *Have hope.* Don't give up no matter how difficult it seems. It is through the power of the indwelling God in you that change and transformation are possible. Love God, and walk in His ways. He will empower you to break free.

THE HOPE

What transformed a man who hated Christians, one who persecuted them with everything in him and who wanted to rid the world of their voice and ways? A God experience! God met this man on the road to Damascus and filled him with the Holy Spirit. This man was Paul. Paul's recognition of Jesus as the fulfillment of prophecy, as Lord of all, was revealed by the Holy Spirit. A God encounter completely changed him forever. Now, filled with compassion and a mission to bring the message of salvation and love to those he hated, he was transformed.

Is change possible? If you have doubt, read about the life of Paul. Through the indwelling of the Holy Spirit in you, He

(God) is able to keep you from falling, to quell the anger and replace it with love. As you are filled with His love, the fruit of His Spirit will become evident in your life—patience, longsuffering, kindness, gentleness, goodness, faithfulness and, yes, self-control. Breaking free from anger is a battle that can be won, but you need God's help. And He is willing to give it. Submit your life totally to Him. Surrender to His love, and see what He does. You will break free from anger.

B R E A K I N G F R E E

P R A Y E R   F O R   Y O U

Thank You, God, that You have given me all that I need to break free from anger. Today I commit this change process to You. And, like Paul, give me a revelation of You that will empower me toward the goal. I want to be transformed for Your glory. Because of You, I can break free!

CHAPTER 1

1. Charles Spielberger quote on anger as quoted by S. F. Duncan (2002), *Dealing With Anger in Relationships*. Retrieved January 31, 2002 from www.montana.edu/wwwpb/pubs/mt2000004.html.

2. S. M. Persons (1997), *Risk Factors Cluster to Harm Health*. Retrieved March 12, 2002 from http://obssr.od.nih.gov/Publications/RISKCLU.HTM.

3. Research from Jeffrey Deffenbacher reported in American Psychological Association (1997). *Psychology in Daily Life: Controlling Anger—Before It Controls You*. Retrieved November 21, 2001 from http://helping.apa.org/daily/anger.html.

4. Ann Moir and David Jessel, *Brain Sex* (New York: Dell Publishing Group, Inc. 1991), 68–87.

CHAPTER 3

1. Directly taken from Logos Research System—Online search for anger instances January 12, 2002, http://wbsa.logos.com/search. *What the Bible Says About...* features The New Nave's Topical Bible, one of over 500 titles available on CD-ROM using Logos

Bible Study Software. Bible references in *What the Bible Says About...* are to The Bible Gateway, copyright © 1996, 1997, 1998, 1999, 2000 Logos Research Systems, Inc.

CHAPTER 5

1. Bushman, Baumeister and Stack, "Catharsis. Aggression and Persuasive Influence: Self-fulfilling or self-defeating prophecies?" *Journal of Personality and Social Psychology,* vol. 76, No. 3 (Jan 1999): 367–376.

CHAPTER 7

1. APA Online. Public Interest Initiatives. *Violence on TV.* Retrieved March 13, 2002 from www.apa.org/pi/pii/vio& tv.html.